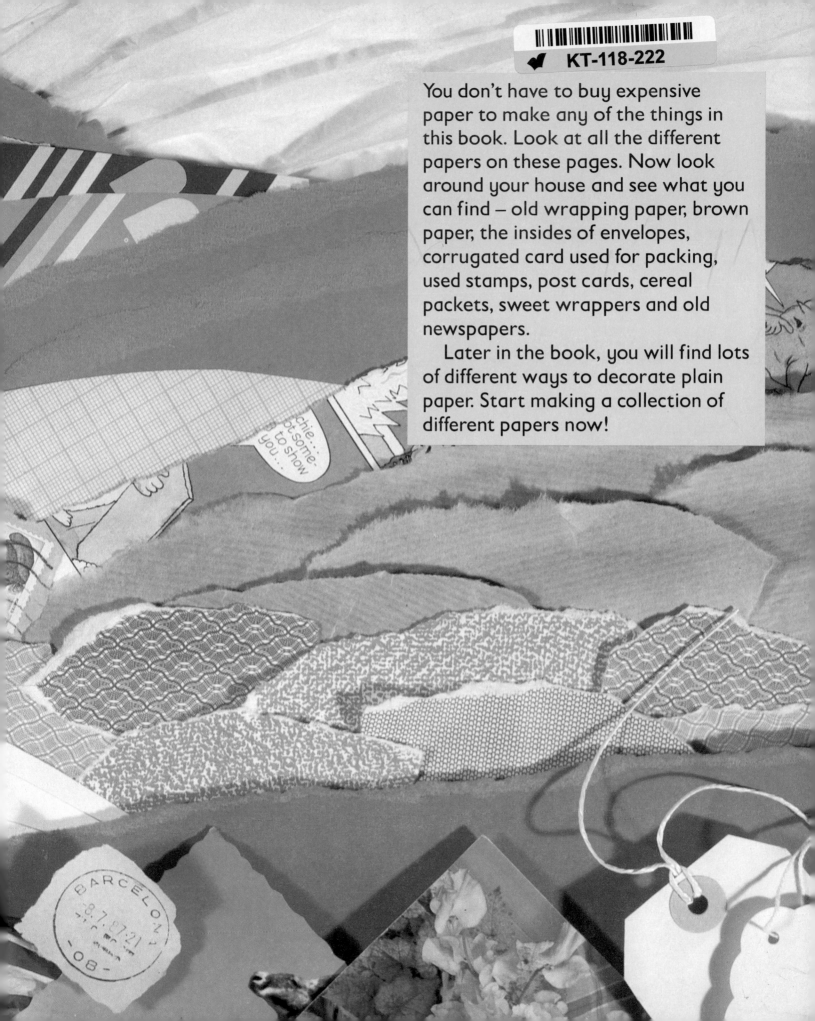

You don't have to buy expensive paper to make any of the things in this book. Look at all the different papers on these pages. Now look around your house and see what you can find – old wrapping paper, brown paper, the insides of envelopes, corrugated card used for packing, used stamps, post cards, cereal packets, sweet wrappers and old newspapers.

Later in the book, you will find lots of different ways to decorate plain paper. Start making a collection of different papers now!

EQUIPMENT

When you have gathered together a collection of different papers, you are almost ready to start! All of the things on these pages are used somewhere in the PAPER book for cutting, gluing, decorating and assembling. You will probably be able to find most of them in your house but you may have to buy some of them from craft or toy shops.

Be very careful when using scissors and craft knives – ask for help if you have any problems with cutting! Always use a piece of thick card or lino when you are cutting with a sharp knife.

straws for splattering and decorating

ruler for straight lines

scissors

paint and brushes for decorating paper

cocktail sticks for flower stems

THE PAPER BOOK

By **HANNAH TOFTS**

Written and Edited by Diane James

Photography by Jon Barnes

CONTENTS

Illustrations by Sally Kindberg

TWO-CAN

BY AIR MAIL
PAR AVION
MIT LUFTPOST
Offres Meublés 4e
MARAIS 5.500 F
MARAIS GD LUXE
RESIDENCE
PORTE DE VINCENNES
USAirmail
Aviation Pioneer
20F

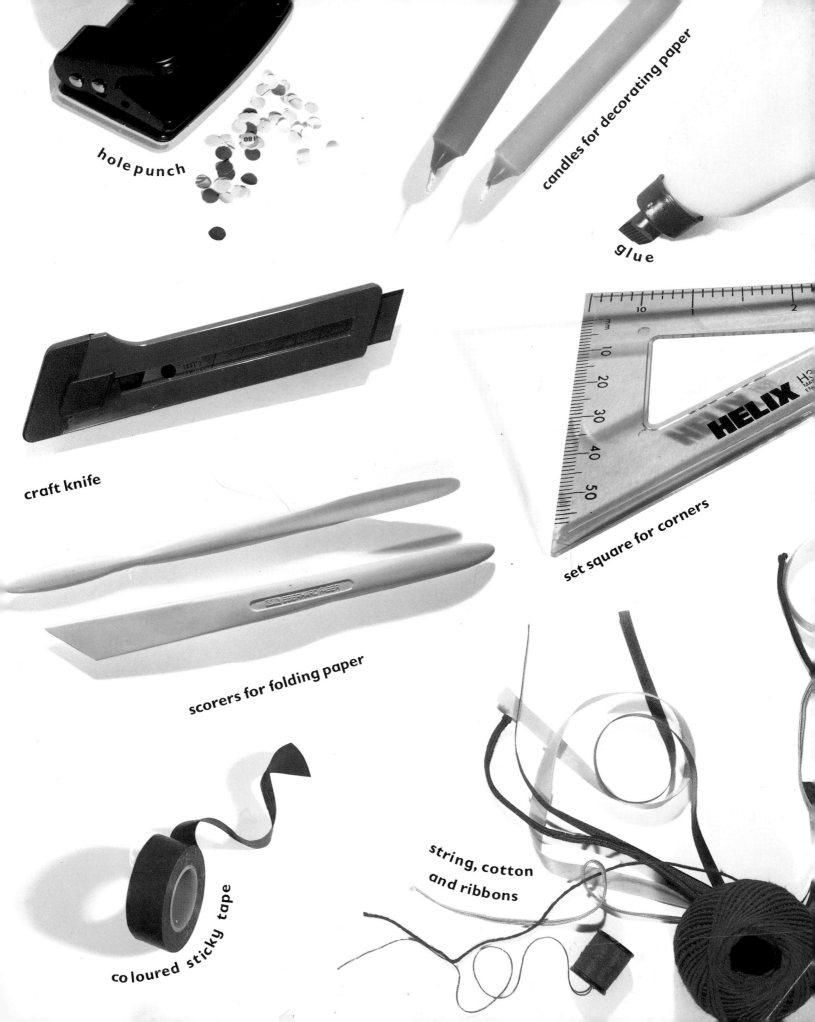

hole punch

candles for decorating paper

glue

craft knife

set square for corners

scorers for folding paper

coloured sticky tape

string, cotton and ribbons

Paper Curls

Cut a long, thin strip of coloured paper. Wrap the strip tightly round a pencil or knitting needle. Pull the pencil or needle out and you will have a paper curl!

Paper Beads

Stick two sheets of coloured paper together. Tear out triangles and roll them up tightly, starting at the wide end.

Crumpled Paper

Give paper an interesting texture by crumpling it up. When you are collecting papers, look for paper that has already been crumpled up.

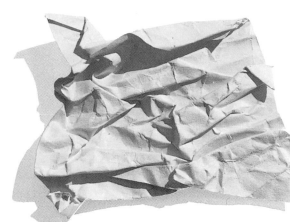

Weaving Paper

Cut out some long, thin strips of different coloured paper. Weave the strips in and out as in the picture. If you want the strips to stay in position, glue them onto a backing sheet.

Stick and Tear

You can make paper stronger by gluing two layers together. If you glue two different colours together and then tear out shapes, you will get an interesting edge. If you stick three or more layers of paper together, you will get an even stronger paper – more like thin card!

Concertina Folds

Take a long, thin strip of paper and practise making concertina folds or pleats. They can be as large or small as you like. Later in this book you will see how to use pleated paper to make jewellery and paper flowers.

Cutting, Punching and Tearing

Cutting paper gives a smooth edge while tearing leaves a ragged edge – both methods give interesting effects and are used in this book. If you have a hole punch, you can punch small, round holes – keep the pieces, they may be useful!

If you look carefully at this picture, you will see that it is made entirely from different papers.

Look around the house to see how many different kinds of paper you can find. The papers here include newspaper, insides of envelopes, brown paper, wrapping paper, greaseproof paper and tissue paper – there are also plastic straws and milk bottle tops!

Draw a rough sketch of your idea and decide which papers will be best.

Cut and tear the papers into shapes and stick them in position, starting with the background.

Remember that you can bend, curl and crumple paper and card to make interesting shapes. Look at pages 6 and 7 to find out how to weave paper and make concertina folds.

Make the paste from the recipe opposite and put some into small containers. Add some powder or poster paint and mix well. Cover a sheet of paper with paste paint. Make cardboard scrapers like the ones at the bottom of the page and use them to make patterns in the paste paint. When the paste paint is dry, you can use the paper to make jewellery, cards, wrapping paper and carrier bags.

Paste Recipe
1. Measure out a mug of flour and three mugs of water.
2. In a saucepan, mix a little of the water with the flour to make a smooth paste.
3. Add the rest of the water and ask a grown-up to heat the mixture until it boils – they must keep stirring all the time! Turn the heat down and let the mixture simmer until the paste thickens. Leave the mixture until it is cold.

Here are some examples of decorated papers using different methods.

Sponge Printing

Try dipping different shaped sponges – large and small – into fairly thick paint. Press the sponge onto the paper.

Object Printing

Look for objects that have an interesting shape or a raised texture. Dip the objects into fairly thick paint and press onto the paper.

Wax and Paint

Make a pattern on the paper with wax crayons or candles. Paint over the wax marks with medium-thick paint. The paint will not stay where the wax marks are.

Crumpled Paper

Crumple up a small piece of paper and dip it into thick paint. Press it onto the paper to make a print.

Splattering

This is a very quick and easy method for decorating paper. Dip a large paint brush into thick paint and either flick or shake it over the paper.

Here are some more methods for decorating papers.

Experiment with the suggestions in this book and try out your own ideas too.

1 & **6** Splatter painting

2 & **9** Crumpled paper printing

3 Crumpled paper – paint a sheet of paper and scrunch it up

4 Sponge printing – try using different types of sponges

5 & **8** Paste paper

7 Wax and paint

10 Sponge and object printing

You don't need any paints or coloured pencils to make these cards and gift tags! All you need is coloured paper, glue, scissors and a craft knife.

Slit and Slot Card

Fold a sheet of coloured paper in half. Make slits from the top to the bottom using a craft knife. Leave a border of at least 1″ (2.5cm) all round the card.

Using different coloured strips of paper, weave them in and out of the slits.

Letter Card and Gift Tag

Paste two sheets of different coloured paper together and fold in half. Using a craft knife, cut the shape of a letter from the front of the card. Keep the letter that you cut out and punch a hole in it. Thread a piece of cord through the hole and you will have a gift tag!

Punch and Tear Card

Paste two sheets of different coloured paper together and fold in half to make a card. Pierce holes in the front of the card with a pencil and tear back strips of paper to make a pattern.

Cut Paper Card

Fold a sheet of coloured paper in half. Using a craft knife, cut wavy slits and wavy shapes in the front of the card. Stick the shapes you cut out back on the front of the card.

Gift Tags

Cut triangles or other shapes from coloured paper. Punch holes in the tops of the triangles or shapes and thread a ribbon through. Write a message on the gift tag and attach it to a present!

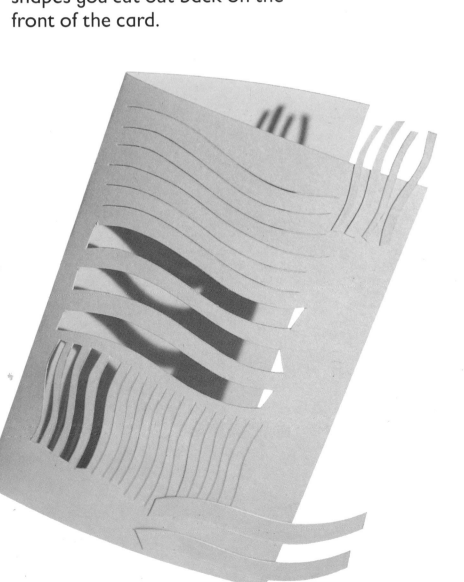

Here is a good way to use some of your decorated papers. When you have wrapped your present, you can add ribbons, bows and flowers to make it look special!

Wrapping a Parcel

Put the present in the middle of the paper. Leave enough overlap at each end so that when you fold the ends over, the present will be covered.

If possible, use double-sided sellotape which will not show.

Try to fold the ends as neatly as possible by making crisp corner folds.

This present has been decorated with a paper curl! Stick two strips of paper together and curl by wrapping round the end of a wooden spoon or a broom handle.

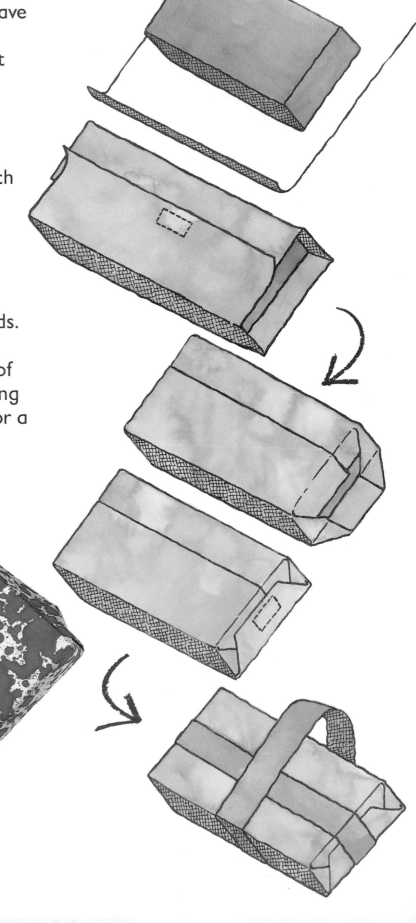

Round Parcels

▲ If you have a present that is an awkward shape, such as a bottle, try putting it in a cardboard tube. Or, wrap corrugated card round it.

Wrap and stick decorated paper round the tube, leaving enough at the ends to fold under. Cut out two circles of paper and stick them over the ends to neaten off.

Make paper curls and a pleated paper bow to decorate the parcel.

Paper Bow and Flower

▼ Make a paper bow to decorate your parcel by cutting thin strips of paper and gluing the ends together. Stick four or more loops together and attach to your parcel. On page 22 you can find out how to make paper flowers.

First decide how big you want your carrier bag to be!

1. On the back of a sheet of decorated paper draw out a plan like the one at the top of the page. The pieces marked 'A' will be the sides of the bag and should be the same measurement. The pieces marked 'B' will be the front and back of the bag and these should also be the same measurement. The pieces marked 'C' should measure just less than the width of 'A'. The front and back should be wider than the sides!

2. Cut out corners and triangles as shown on the illustration. Use a scoring tool to score all the lines marked. The height of the triangles to be scored – marked 'X'– should be equal to half the width of the sides of the bag – also marked 'X'.

3. Fold over and glue the top of the bag. This makes a strong, neat edge.

4. You can either use a hole punch to punch holes for cord at the top of the bag (front and back), or you can make small slits to thread ribbon through.

I.

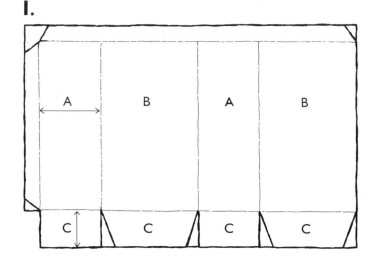

2.

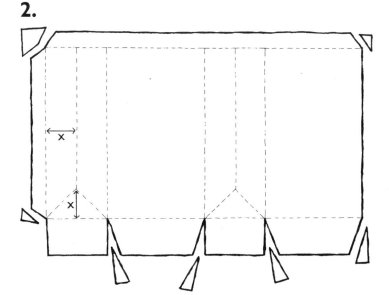

3.

4.

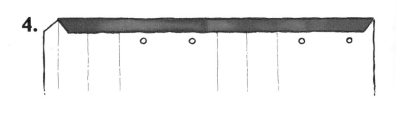

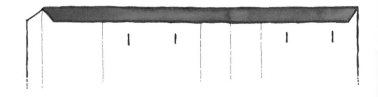

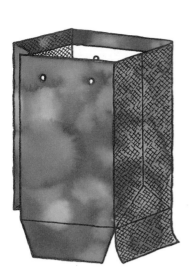

▲ Glue the bag together at the flap edge.

▲ Fold the bottom flaps under and glue.

▲ Gently push in the sides along the scored lines.

◀ Slot cord or ribbon through the holes for handles.

Here are some suggestions for making paper flowers – but try your own ideas too!

Pleat a strip of coloured paper. Pinch one end together and stick a strip of paper round to hold it.

Cut a long strip of coloured paper. Make cuts along the length as in the illustration. Roll up the paper and bend the petals back. Try using different coloured papers. Add leaves and a stem.

To make stems for your paper flowers, wrap a thin strip of green paper round a cocktail stick. Glue or tape the ends. You could also use a straw cut into short lengths and painted green.

Cut out different shapes for leaves – long and thin, short and pointed. Score down the centre of the leaf and fold. Leaves are good for covering up joins between flowers and stems!

This 'petal' flower was made by cutting separate coloured petals, overlapping them and sticking them together. The paper curls were made by wrapping thin strips of paper round a pencil.

Cut petal shapes in a long strip of paper as in the illustration. Roll the flower up and fold back the petals. Tissue paper makes good roses. Try making the petals different shapes.

▲ Woven Ear-rings

Cut some thin strips of different coloured papers. Weave the strips in and out. When you have made a woven square, cut out a piece of paper the same size and glue them together. Glue an ear-ring attachment to the back.

▼ Pleated Brooch

Cut out two paper triangles. Pleat the triangles like the ones in the illustration. Glue the long edges together. Pinch the pleats together in the middle. Wrap and glue a thin strip of paper round the middle to hold the pleats in place. Glue a brooch attachment to the back.

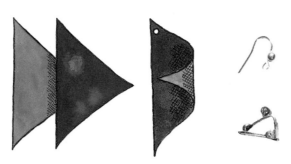

▲ Triangle Ear-rings

Glue two different coloured triangles together. Curl the triangle round the handle of a wooden spoon. Pierce a small hole at the top of two triangles and thread an ear-ring attachment through.

▼ Concertina Bracelet

Take two long strips of paper. Glue the ends together at right angles. Continue folding one piece over the other as in the illustration. Glue the ends together. Because concertina folds stretch, you should be able to slip the bracelet over your wrist easily.

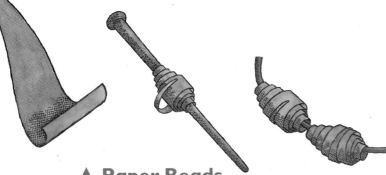

▲ Paper Beads

Cut out a long, thin paper triangle. Starting at the wide end, roll the triangle round a knitting needle. Pull the needle out. Make a collection of beads and string them onto coloured cord.

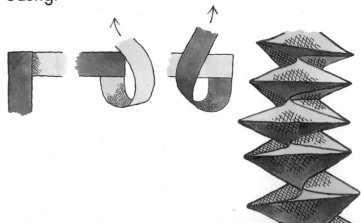

You should be able to find ear-ring attachments in craft shops. You may also find hair slides which you can stick paper bows or flowers to.

Papier Mâché means 'Paper Pulp'. You make it by building up layers of pasted paper.

First you will need to tear up lots of strips of paper – newspaper and coloured paper. Use the 'Paste Recipe' from page 10.

You can use your fingers to cover the strips of paper with paste, but an old paint brush is less messy!

Making a Bowl

1. Cover a ball with plenty of vaseline. This will make the bowl easier to get off.

2. Paste on the inside layer of torn paper using lots of paste on both sides of the paper. Do not go more than half way up the ball or the bowl will not come off!

3. Paste on 6 or 7 layers of paper to make the ball firm. Try to keep the layers even.

4. When the paper is dry, ask a grown-up to help cut round the edge of the bowl and gently lift it off.

You can use all sorts of things as basic moulds to cover with papier mâché. Large and small balls make good bowls but you can also use paper or plastic cups, trays or plates.

Whatever you use, cover it well with vaseline first. This will make it easier to take the papier mâché off when it is dry.

You can decorate papier mâché by painting it when it is dry, or by using a pattern of coloured paper for the final layer. If you are making a bowl, remember that the first layer you paste down will be the inside of the bowl!

These fish don't need feeding and you can make them any colour you like! If you can't find a goldfish bowl, an old fish tank or a large glass jar will work just as well. Look at the instructions on the next page.

Turn the container upside down onto a piece of card and draw round the edge. Cut out the shape. Use sticky tape to attach different lengths of cotton to the fish and to the cardboard top. Put the top over the bowl and watch your fish swimming around!

Cut some simple fish shapes out of coloured card. Using a craft knife, cut patterns in the fish or use a pencil to punch holes. Try sticking different coloured card behind the cut-out shapes.

You can make watery shapes by using the insides of envelopes, and strips of curled paper make good seaweed!